King Ludwig's Castle

Germany's Neuschwanstein

By Lisa Trumbauer

Consultant: Stephen F. Brown,
Director, Institute of Medieval Philosophy and Theology, Boston College

BEARPORT
PUBLISHING COMPANY, INC.

New York, New York

Credits

Cover, Douglas Armand / Alamy; title page, Douglas Armand / Alamy.

Background (throughout), V&A Images / Alamy; (Ludwig II), CORBIS; 4-5, CORBIS; 8-9, Todd Dacquisto / Index Stock; 9, Matteo Del Grosso / Alamy; 10, CORBIS; 11, The Granger Collection, New York; 12-13, Historische Ansichtskarten; 13, Lebrecht Music and Arts Photo Library / Alamy; 14, The Granger Collection, New York; 15, Mary Evans Picture Library; 16-17(both), AKG-Images; 18, Bayerische Verwaltung der staatlichen Schlösser, Gärten und Seen / Neuschwanstein Castle Photo Library; 19(top), Ric Erherbright; 19(bottom), Richard Nowitz; 20, Adam Woolfitt / CORBIS; 21, Bayerische Verwaltung der staatlichen Schlösser, Gärten und Seen / Neuschwanstein Castle Photo Library; 22-23, Hulton Deutsch Collection / CORBIS; 23, Getty Images; 24(t), The London Times, June, 1886 / NI Syndication Limited; 24(b), 25, Clipart.com; 26, Dennis Hallinan / Alamy; 26-27, Rodica Prato; 29, Douglas Armand / Alamy.

Design and production by Dawn Beard Creative, Triesta Hall of Blu-Design, and Octavo Design and Production, Inc.

Library of Congress Cataloging-in-Publication Data

Trumbauer, Lisa, 1963-
  King Ludwig's castle: Germany's Neuschwanstein / by Lisa Trumbauer; consultant, Stephen Brown.
    p. cm. — (Castles, palaces & tombs)
  Includes index.
  ISBN 1-59716-002-4 (lib. bdg.) — ISBN 1-59716-025-3 (pbk.)
  1. Schloss Neuschwanstein (Germany) — Juvenile literature. 2. Ludwig, II, King of Bavaria, 1845-1886 — Palaces — Germany — Bavaria — Juvenile literature. I. Title. II. Series.

  DD901.N579T78 2005
  943'.3081'092—dc22

                    2004020990

For more information, write to Bearport Publishing Company, Inc., 101 Fifth Avenue, Suite 6R, New York, New York 10003. Printed in the United States of America.

1 2 3 4 5 6 7 8 9 10

Table of Contents

King Ludwig Leaves His Castle

The silent villagers walked up the mountain trail. They stopped at a small brick gatehouse. They looked up the mountain. There stood Neuschwanstein (noi-SHVAHN-stine) Castle. White, stone walls dotted with windows glowed against the sky. Round, pointed towers rose up in the air.

Suddenly, the gates opened. The crowd parted to make room for a carriage. Through a window, the villagers saw the sad face of King Ludwig II. He had been arrested. Government **officials** thought he was crazy. He didn't know it, but King Ludwig would never see his **beloved** castle again.

Disney's famous Magic Kingdom castle was modeled after Neuschwanstein Castle.

A Young Prince

Prince Ludwig II was born on August 25, 1845. His parents were the king and queen of Bavaria. Since Ludwig was the oldest son, he would one day become king. His parents kept him from the outside world to protect him from danger.

PACIFIC
OCEAN

NORTH
AMERICA

N
W   E
S

SOUTH
AMERICA

Ludwig spent a lot of time alone. He often invented his own games. Sometimes he pretended he was king. He liked to order his younger brother Otto around. Once, Ludwig made believe that Otto was a prisoner and tied him up. A **servant** finally set Otto free when he found the frightened boy.

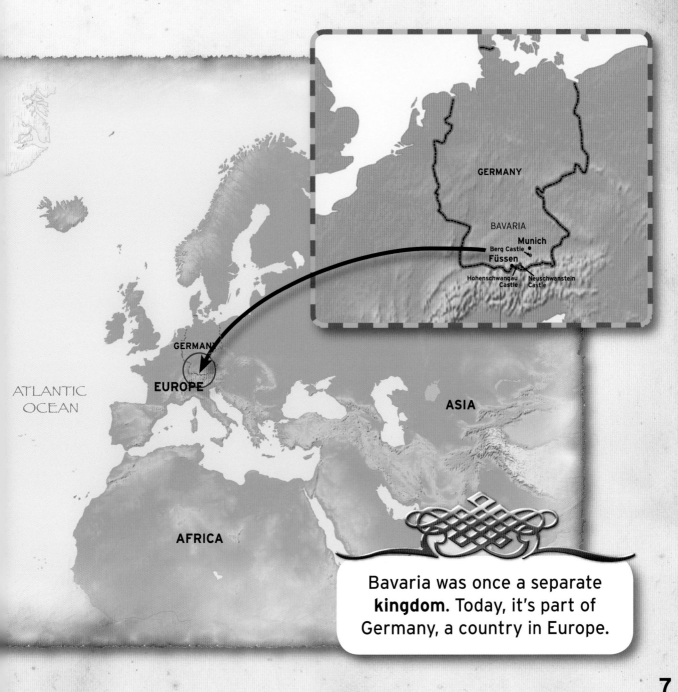

Bavaria was once a separate **kingdom.** Today, it's part of Germany, a country in Europe.

Ludwig's Childhood Castle

The young Ludwig loved stories. He read every book he could find. He liked to read **fantasy** stories and history books. He also read about ancient kingdoms, brave **knights**, and old castles. Ludwig really loved Lohengrin (LOE-en-grin), a story about a swan that turned into a German prince.

Hohenschwangau Castle

When not reading, Ludwig loved to play in the mountains. His family spent vacations in their mountain castle called Hohenschwangau. (hoe-en-SHVAHN-gow). This huge stone **fortress** was built in the 1100s. Paintings of Bavarian knights covered the walls. Ludwig learned about Bavarian history through these paintings.

The mountains near Hohenschwangau Castle at dusk

Lohengrin was the name of a famous **opera** by Richard Wagner.

Ludwig Becomes King

Ludwig's carefree childhood ended when his father died on March 10, 1864. Two days later, Ludwig became the king of Bavaria. He was only eighteen years old.

Ludwig dressed in a blue army uniform with silver buttons, ribbons, and medals. The guards raised their swords in salute. Ludwig said the **oath** that made him king.

Ludwig, soon after he became king

Many people from Bavaria had never seen Ludwig before. They were struck by the young, handsome man. They were moved when he held back tears as he became king. The people loved their new king.

King Ludwig, age 19, in 1865

Ludwig was nicknamed "The Swan King."

Bavaria Goes to War

After Ludwig became king, war broke out in Europe. The kingdom of Prussia warned of an attack on Bavaria. Ludwig wanted peace, but he could not prevent war. Instead of fighting, the young king ran away to Berg Castle outside of Munich. He thought he would be safe there.

Berg Castle

When Prussia finally **declared** war on Bavaria, officials searched for King Ludwig. They tracked him down at Berg Castle where he was found in a dark room reading poetry out loud. He was dressed in costume as the swan prince, Lohengrin.

Lohengrin

The war against Prussia lasted seven weeks in the summer of 1866.

A New Castle

Ludwig didn't like being king. He found it boring. He also didn't like Munich, the city where the king was supposed to live. Ludwig liked the mountains, where he often escaped to Hohenschwangau Castle.

A view of Munich, Germany in 1822

Ludwig dreamed of building his own castle. He wanted something bigger than Hohenschwangau. Ludwig chose a spot high in the mountains for his new home. He decided to build a place that he thought the swan prince would like. Ludwig called his dream castle Neuschwanstein.

King Ludwig dressed in his royal robes

In English, Neuschwanstein means "new swan stone."

The Castle's Construction

Ludwig began building the castle in 1869. It was a huge job. Workers built a road up the mountain to carry large equipment and tools. Then they had to move heavy stone and wood 600 feet up into the mountains. Ludwig's workers used modern equipment to make the job easier. A **crane** powered by steam lifted material up to the castle.

For water, workers laid pipes from a narrow **gorge** up in the mountains. The water rushing down the mountain built up enough **pressure** to pump the water through the whole castle.

King Ludwig died while the castle was being built.

A Modern Castle

From the outside, Ludwig's building looked like an old German knight's castle. Inside, his new home was modern. Ludwig had a telephone system to talk with servants. He put in an elevator to make it easy to carry meals from the kitchen to the dining hall above. He also put in central heating to warm the many rooms.

The kitchen at Neuschwanstein Castle

The castle was also famous for its modern plumbing system. Hot and cold water flowed through pipes on every floor. The bathrooms even had automatic flush toilets.

Hot and cold water flowed through this "swan" faucet at the castle.

The salon with pictures from the opera *Lohengrin* on the walls

Ludwig spent all his money building three new castles. Neuschwanstein was his favorite.

A King Without a Kingdom

As Ludwig built Neuschwanstein, his kingdom of Bavaria fell. In 1871, Bavaria and several other kingdoms became the single country of Germany. Ludwig kept the title of king. He, however, no longer had a kingdom to rule.

King Ludwig's bedroom

Ludwig now spent all his time on Neuschwanstein. He ordered **designers** to craft beautiful rooms. Painters, sculptors, and artists turned rooms into works of art. Fourteen wood carvers spent four years making the wooden bed in Ludwig's bedroom. One room was made to look like the inside of a cave.

The cave room had rock walls, colored lights, and water fountains.

Has Ludwig Gone Crazy?

Building the castle took a lot of money. Ludwig didn't have enough to complete the job. He began asking other countries for money to finish his dream castle. People in Germany were worried. They feared that the king had become a **beggar**.

The Reichstag, a government building in Germany

The German government said that King Ludwig was crazy. A group of doctors and officials were sent to Neuschwanstein to arrest him. The king had no choice but to go with them. His dream to spend the rest of his life in the castle ended.

King Ludwig, just before his death

Villagers who lived near Ludwig's castle loved him until the end. As he left, they threw flowers at his carriage.

Ludwig's Strange Death

Ludwig was taken to Berg Castle. It was turned into a special prison hospital just for him. Two days later, Ludwig and a doctor went for a walk. When they did not return within a few hours, officials sent out a search party. They found the bodies of Ludwig and his doctor floating in a lake.

THE TIMES, TUESDAY, JUNE 15, 1886

LATEST INTELLIGENCE.

◆

(FROM OUR CORRESPONDENTS.)

SUICIDE OF THE KING OF BAVARIA.

VIENNA, June 14.

King Louis of Bavaria has committed suicide. The bodies of His Majesty and of Dr. Gudden, his medical a̶ ̶... ̶ ̶n̶i̶g̶h̶t̶ ̶i̶n̶ ̶t̶h̶e̶ Starnberg ̶... ̶ animation ̶...

as, owing to the holid appeared since Sunday ment created great const.

The news of the trag Bavaria has naturally Berlin, as everywhere e fortunately for the gra by details of the occ keeping its Whitsuntid meagro fly-sheets are streets with the annou at the la ng left S

King Ludwig was loved by the Bavarian people. Many of them attended his funeral.

No one saw what happened. The deaths caused much talk. Some people said the king was killed by German officials. Others said Ludwig killed his doctor, and then took his own life. We may never know the truth.

King Ludwig's funeral procession

After Ludwig was taken to Berg Castle, his uncle took over as king.

Visiting King Ludwig's Castle Today

Seven weeks after King Ludwig died, his fairytale castle opened to the public. Today, the castle is one of Germany's most popular tourist sites.

To reach Neuschwanstein, most people fly to Munich, Germany. The castle is about 80 miles southwest of the city. Visitors can drive or take a train to the town of Füssen (FOO-sen). Then they can take a bus or walk to the village of Hohenschwangau. From there, the castle is a 30-minute walk up a **steep** path. At the castle, visitors may join tours to see the 15 amazing rooms that are open to the public.

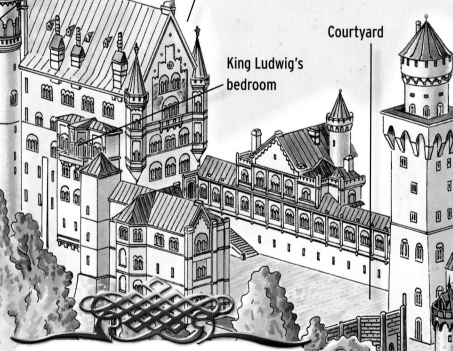

The Throne Hall is on the top two floors.

The Cave Room and the Salon are on the third floor.

Courtyard

King Ludwig's bedroom

Main entrance and Gatehouse

More than a million people visit Neuschwanstein every year. In the summer, about 6,000 visitors a day come to the castle.

Just the Facts

- The only people who lived with King Ludwig at Neuschwanstein were his servants. He had more than 20 servants taking care of him.

- Ludwig once ordered his servants to prepare a feast for a very important guest: his horse.

- Ludwig tried to build three castles. Only one, Linderhof (LIN-der-hof), was fully completed. A fourth was being planned at the time of his death.

- Neuschwanstein appeared in the 1968 movie *Chitty Chitty Bang Bang*. In the movie, it was the home of Baron Bomburst.

- Throne Hall was not completed when King Ludwig died, and the castle still doesn't have a throne.

Timeline

1866
The Seven Week War
with Prussia begins.

1871
Bavaria becomes part of the
single nation of Germany.

1845
Ludwig is born.

1840   1860   1880   1900

1886
King Ludwig dies.

1869
Ludwig starts to build
Neuschwanstein Castle.

1864
Ludwig's father
dies. Ludwig is made
king of Bavaria.

Glossary

beggar (BEG-ur) a person who asks someone for help, especially for money or food

beloved (bi-LUHV-id) greatly loved

crane (KRANE) a machine with a tall arm used to lift and move heavy objects

declared (di-KLAIRD) announced in a formal way

designers (di-ZINE-urz) people who plan and decorate rooms

fantasy (FAN-tuh-see) characters, places, or events that are imagined and are not likely to happen in real life

fortress (FOR-truss) a large building or area that is strengthened against attacks

gorge (GORJ) a narrow space between rocky cliffs

kingdom (KING-duhm) a country that has a king or queen as its ruler

knights (NITES) soldiers who fought on horseback during the Middle Ages (which occurred between the years 500–1540)

oath (OHTH) a serious promise

officials (uh-FISH-uhlz) people who hold an office or important position

opera (OP-ur-uh) a play in which all or most of the words are sung and the music is played by an orchestra

pressure (PRESH-ur) the force made by pressing on something

servant (SUR-vuhnt) a person, such as a maid or a cook, who works in another person's house doing housework, cooking, or other chores

steep (STEEP) having a sharp slope or slant

Bibliography

Knapp, Gottfried, and Achim Bunz. *Neuschwanstein.* London, England: Axel Menges (2000).

Prestel. *Neuschwanstein (Prestel Museum Guides Compact).* Prestel Publishing (2001).

Read More

Kruckmann, Peter O. *The King and His Castle.* Munich, Germany: Prestel Verlag (2001).

Learn More Online

Visit these Web sites to learn more about Neuschwanstein Castle:

www.castles.org/castles/Europe/Central_Europe/Germany/germany7.htm

www.germanworld.com/neu.htm

www.neuschwanstein.de/english/castle/

Index

About the Author

Lisa Trumbauer is the author of over 200 books for children. She's an avid traveler who has visited Neuschwanstein Castle several times. It's only a half-hour drive from her grandmother's home in Bavaria. Lisa lives in New Jersey with her husband, Dave, their dog Blue, and two cats named Cosmo and Cleo. Lisa can be reached via her Web site at www.lisatrumbauer.com.